SHOWING UP

SHOWING UP

How the Power of Presence Is Reshaping Evangelism

Kerry Willis
and
Margaret Michael
with Brian Charette

THE FOUNDRY
PUBLISHING

The Foundry Publishing
PO Box 419527
Kansas City, MO 64141
thefoundrypublishing.com

978-0-8341-3834-6

Printed in the
United States of America

Cover designer: Arthur Cherry
Interior designer: Sharon Page

Library of Congress Cataloging-in-Publication Data
Names: Willis, Kerry W., 1961- author. | Michael, Margaret, 1967- author.
Title: Showing up : how the power of presence is reshaping evangelism / Kerry Willis and
    Margaret Michael with Brian Charette.
Description: Kansas City, MO : The Foundry Publishing, 2019. | Summary: "The authors
    challenge those interested in evangelism to shift from procedures and formulas to true
    connections and real relationships. They demonstrate that we don't have to be academic
    theologians or dynamic crusaders to be faithful witnesses to the gospel of Jesus Christ"—
    Provided by publisher.
Identifiers: LCCN 2019033208 (print) | LCCN 2019033209 (ebook) | ISBN 9780834138346 |
    ISBN 9780834138353 (ebook)
Subjects: LCSH: Witness bearing (Christianity) | Interpersonal relations—Religious aspects—
    Christianity. | Evangelistic work.
Classification: LCC BV4520 .W525 2019 (print) | LCC BV4520 (ebook) | DDC 269/.2—dc23
LC record available at https://lccn.loc.gov/2019033208
LC ebook record available at https://lccn.loc.gov/2019033209

10 9 8 7 6 5 4 3 2 1

*King Jesus, as our inheritance, you have
filled the sanctuaries of our everyday lives
with the holiness of your presence.*

———————❖———————

*Empower us now to be light and to shine so that we might
bring your inheritance of lost souls to you, finally found.*

———————❖———————

We dedicate this project to presence, unity, and love.

CONTENTS

ACKNOWLEDGMENTS

Kerry

I am a debtor to God the Father, God the Son, God the Holy Spirit—one. The holy inheritance, the presence of my God within me—I humbly but surely claim him as my life and light on earth and for eternity. Holy presence really is everything to me; it's true that presence matters most!

I am indebted to my precious family: Kim, Grayson, Allison, and Joshua. I desire to be loved, appreciated, and respected most by you, my closest beloved ones. I cherish each of you with my whole heart. Thank you for loving me so undeniably and unconditionally. Together, let us love Jesus passionately and always seek to be sacred sanctuaries of his presence. *Deo volente*—as God wills.

I am also indebted to my Christlike friends and co-authors: Pastor Margaret Michael and Dr. Brian Charette. Without your unbridled encouragement and unrivaled excellence, this "presence project" might have remained locked away in my soul rather than becoming an inspiration to other souls. I believe in you and the one who is in you. You are something else.

Margaret

I am most grateful to the Lord who pursued me when I was lost; I am grateful that he made the way for my salvation and that he gave the precious gift of the Holy Spirit. I'm so grateful for the Lord's presence in my life, and I am deeply humbled that he would use the likes of me to carry his presence to others.

My heart is filled with gratitude for my family: Steve, Sydney, Olivia, and Adam. Thank you for your continuous love and support over the years. You have taught me so much about the power of presence, especially in the context of our home.

To Pastor Kerry Willis, who in 1996 took time to answer my questions about faith, and later led me into a saving relationship with Jesus Christ: My life was forever changed because you were present for me in my moment of crisis. Thank you for always encouraging me beyond what I could envision for myself. I am truly grateful.

To Dr. Brian Charette: Thank you for taking the time to listen, share your thoughts, and help me work through the concepts and grasp the vision of this book so that we could bring it together for the glory of God and the work of his kingdom.

FOREWORD

If you want to bring non-Christian friends to Christ, it is absolutely essential that you build relationships with them. Those who are far from God are usually also far from the church, and for the most part, nonbelievers are isolated from the Christian message: they don't watch Christian television or listen to Christian radio; they don't read tracts left in bathrooms or attend conferences and revivals. Rather, nonbelievers are most likely to be reached through relationship. Of course, that is by design: relationship is at the heart of the Trinity of Father, Son, and Holy Spirit. By extension, relationship is folded into our being as bearers of God's image.

Interestingly enough, the unchurched also recognize the primacy of relationships. In recent research by the Barna Group, nonbelievers were asked, "What would encourage you to attend a church?" Out of seven possible choices, which included options such as advertising and marketing, one answer rose to the top: *the invitation of a friend*. Nonbelievers themselves acknowledge that in order to hear the gospel, they need someone to venture into their world and build a relational bridge.

Thus, the first step in leading someone to Christ is to reach out to the people in our sphere of influence through the ministry of presence. Rather than beginning with a gospel tract or presenting step-by-step plans to salvation, we begin by building credibility through personal connections. Most people are far more inclined to consider a life-changing message from a trusted friend than from a stranger or casual acquaintance.

The Christians who practice regular acts of kindness, cultivate friendships through hospitality, and manifest the unconditional love of Christ at all times are the ones who have the greatest influence on others. This is what the apostle Paul addressed in Colossians 4, when he encouraged the early Christians to fill their conversations with grace and season their words with salt. It is the combination of warm love and generous grace that prepares hearts to receive the gospel seed.

In these pages, Kerry Willis and Margaret Michael have provided a practical, yet profound guide to "presence evangelism." They remind us that when Christ is in us, people cannot help but be impacted. The authors' emphasis on being, rather than mere doing, is based on the truth that a faithful, loving presence will do more to draw people to Christ than anything else.

In inviting you to read this book and put its time-honored wisdom into practice, we also invite you into a new world of meaningful relationships with eternal results.

David A. Busic
General Superintendent, Church of the Nazarene

INTRODUCTION

We are writing this book because we've seen the struggle—the struggle that comes with living life in our time. Lonely people crave relationships, but often lack true connection. We see those who are desperate for hope never find it and choose an empty substitute in food, alcohol, or drugs. Even in the church, there are some who put on their best face on Sunday morning, but find it difficult to face the world on Monday.

We see the practice of hospitality, the discipline of connection, and the art of real friendship under siege. Where true connection and caring are so desperately needed, we see isolation. We invent new technologies, new social networks, that promise deeper connection. But those often become barriers rather than bridges. People hurry. People hide. People hurt.

There is an answer, of course—his name is Jesus Christ. He is the one, last, and lasting hope for mankind; the Lord and giver of life; the light for a dark world.

And that brings us to another struggle at the heart of this book: believers' struggle with the Great Commission. We know what the Bible says about reaching the lost:

> "So wherever you go, make disciples of all nations: Baptize them in the name of the Father, and of the Son, and of the Holy Spirit. Teach them to do everything I have commanded you." (Matthew 28:19–20)

"But you will receive power when the Holy Spirit comes to you. Then you will be my witnesses to testify about me in Jerusalem, throughout Judea and Samaria, and to the ends of the earth." (Acts 1:8)

"But dedicate your lives to Christ as Lord. Always be ready to defend your confidence in God when anyone asks you to explain it. However, make your defense with gentleness and respect." (1 Peter 3:15)

We know that we are called to be his witnesses, to tell our friends and neighbors about Jesus, to—dare we say it?—*evangelize*. We don't see it as optional, but many see it as excruciating. In some church circles, the word "evangelism" conjures up thoughts of door-to-door cold calls or sales-like closing techniques. For some, witnessing means rejection, embarrassment, and putting our reputation on the line. While we understand that risking rejection, embarrassment, and reputation for the gospel may be necessary, we also believe that our enemy has used those anxieties to keep people rooted in their pews on Sunday mornings so that they hardly ever venture out of their comfort zones.

That is the struggle that motivated this book, and the battle we wish to engage. We believe there is a biblical model for evangelism that every believer can embrace regardless of personality, background, or spiritual gifting. We won't claim this model is easy, but it is from God, and it will result in the increase of his kingdom— and likely, the increase of your local church too.

As we write, we are making some assumptions about you. In fact, we've been praying for you along these lines:

Assumption #1: That you are in a right relationship with God—that is, that you are pursuing an intimate and committed relationship with Jesus Christ and answering the call to holiness. (You can't give love to others if you haven't received God's love yourself.)

Assumption #2: That <u>you are willing</u> to <u>reach others</u>; that you <u>want</u> <u>to build friendships</u> <u>with people</u> who haven't <u>made a commitment</u> <u>to Christ</u>.

yes, help me Lord

Assumption #3: That in those relationships, <u>you desire to love</u> and influence; that you see Christ's call to love others as supreme; that <u>loving your neighbor as yourself isn't optional for you.</u>

Assumption #4: That <u>you are open to telling your story</u> when the <u>Lord calls</u> you to share it with a friend or family member.

So, with those assumptions, we are introducing a model for evangelism that centers on the idea of *presence*. Presence is certainly not a new concept—its roots are in God's Word. However, it is a way of life that needs reviving. Simply stated, the idea behind this model is that, by <u>recognizing and acting on opportunities</u> to be present in your relationships, you can become the evangelist you never *yes* thought you could be. The reason for this is simple: presence makes you <u>an influencer</u>. <u>The Spirit's work within you is all you need to</u> <u>change the world</u>. <u>If you are willing for Christ to reach the lost</u> *yes i* <u>through you</u>, he will. In fact, the heart of this book can be found *am.* in this single statement: <u>The main purpose of our lives must be to</u> *willing* <u>serve as carriers of the presence of Christ and to make a way for</u> <u>him to manifest himself through us.</u>

At a time like this, people are counting on Christ in us.

Pastor Kerry Willis
Pastor Margaret Michael

❖

Let us wait in silence until we are
aware of the presence of Jesus
with and within us, without
which we will experience no
rest for our souls, no power for
our lives, no joy for our hearts,
and no peace for our minds.
The secret of Christ's presence
within us is this:
eternal heavenly treasures are
secured in our earthly lives,
beginning now.

❖

1
IN YOU

—❖—

You can't really be present to others without God's presence in you; that's where it all starts. This is reflected in Colossians 1:27, which includes one of the most beautiful promises in the Bible: God wants people all over to know him, to hope in him. And he does it through Jesus living in you by his Spirit. Only Christ's presence in you empowers you to be present with others.

That's why John 15:5 is such an important foundation for our understanding of presence: "I am the vine. You are the branches. Those who live in me while I live in them will produce a lot of fruit. But you can't produce anything without me." Apart from Christ, we don't have much of anything to offer those around us. Again, this is how presence begins: by Christ living in you and supplying all that you need to be the person he has called you to be.

If you pay close attention to the story of Gideon, you might notice that it features somewhat strange imagery. We already know Gideon—God's unlikely hero from the book of Judges. In the story, God's people had turned from him (again) and were being threatened by the Midianites. That's when God called Gideon, who was threshing wheat in an attempt to hide it from the enemy.

The Lord turned to him and said, "You will rescue Israel from Midian with the strength you have. I am sending you."

Gideon said to him, "Excuse me, sir! How can I rescue Israel? Look at my whole family. It's the weakest one in Manasseh. And me? I'm the least important member of my family."

The Lord replied, "I will be with you. You will defeat Midian as if it were only one man."

(Judges 6:14–16)

Later, with the battle approaching and armies gathering, Judges 6:34 reveals the key to Israel and Gideon's victory: "Then the Lord's Spirit gave Gideon strength." But as we see in the Jubilee translation, there is more happening here than a simple imparting of power: "And the Spirit of the LORD clothed himself in Gideon" (Judges 6:34, JUB). According to the Brown-Driver-Briggs Hebrew lexicon, this is the most accurate translation of the original Hebrew. God's presence in Gideon is so strong that it's as if he were *wearing* Gideon. On the outside, we see the Little Wheat Thresher That Could—but this is only the "clothing." On the inside is God, and he wears Gideon like a garment. God's presence was the source of Gideon's power, and it's the source of yours too.

When it comes to reaching the lost around you, can you imagine God wearing *you* like clothing? In this scenario, you are still the one working to build meaningful relationships with your family, friends and community. However, the power and the presence come from the Lord within you. And from there, like Gideon, you see things you never imagined. It's not you, a lone superhero, accomplishing the impossible through your strength and cunning; rather, it's you surrendering to God, inviting him to take hold of your life and live in you. That is indeed the hope of glory.

One of the challenges of evangelism is that it has sometimes felt too dependent on the evangelist, as though witnessing were an individual pursuit—you against the world. No wonder so many Christians have found it daunting. When it comes to presence, the "secret" to reaching others is not in the struggling, but in the surrendering.

We think this is what Paul is getting at in Galatians 2:20 when he writes, "I no longer live, but Christ lives in me. The life I now live I live by believing in God's Son, who loved me and took the punishment for my sins." Perhaps we become so frustrated with our worship, our prayer, service, and evangelism because we are striving to work *for* God, straining against obstacles to try and try and try with precious little to show for it. But effectiveness is more about his presence than our planning, more about his grace than our guts.

God's presence and power become the engine for all we do in Christ—the service, the prayer, the worship, the good deeds, the evangelism. As Paul reminds us in Philippians 2:13, "It is God who produces in you the desires and actions that please him." Jesus himself prayed about this presence before he made his great sacrifice: "I have made you known to them, and will continue to make you known in order that the love you have for me may be in them and that I myself may be in them" (John 17:26, NIV). And then, when he rose again, Jesus promised this same presence to his disciples: "But you will receive power when the Holy Spirit comes to you. Then you will be my witnesses to testify about me in Jerusalem, throughout Judea and Samaria, and to the ends of the earth" (Acts 1:8).

If you're weary of and frustrated by falling short when it comes to prayer, devotion, and reaching the lost, this is good news! It's not about you and it never has been. It's not about clinging to the rope with blistered hands in a spiritual tug-of-war, or doing your best and failing miserably. No—presence evangelism is about falling to your knees and kneeling at the feet of Jesus, admitting your frailties and proclaiming your need for him.

In the end, Jesus isn't looking for followers. He's looking for sanctuaries—disciples who will reflect his presence, power, and love to all around them. When Christ is in you, it's difficult for people *not* to be

God's presence and power
become the engine for all we
do in Christ—the service, the
prayer, the worship, the good
deeds, the evangelism.

impacted by your presence. That's how we define presence evangelism: it's a lifestyle of manifesting Christ to the people around you.

That's Elaine's story. Elaine is a precious senior citizen who lives in an
assisted living facility and doesn't get to come to church very often.
But I (Kerry) remember one Easter when Elaine's granddaughter
brought her to the service—they sat toward the back as I preached,
both smiling broadly. At the end of the service, Elaine's granddaughter pulled me aside and told me that her grandmother wanted me to
know something very important: "Grandma Elaine wanted me to tell
you that she can't hear a word you're saying," her granddaughter said.
"But she loves to come whenever she can just to sit and look at the
countenance of the presence of God on your face."

Immediately, I knew that what Elaine had seen wasn't the result
of anything I had done. It was something I *couldn't* have done even
if I had tried. But God does things we can't even know about; he
works *through* us because of his presence *in* us. That's the idea of
God wearing you like a garment: people see you, but the presence
of God pours out through the stitching, the seams, and the smiles.
From a practical standpoint, this means we enter the world of presence evangelism from a kneeling position.

I (Margaret) was preparing for our church's local outreach at the
annual county fair. We were planning to host a booth called The
Resting Place, where people could come and sit, no strings attached. It's an unusual approach to fair exhibits, we admit. We
simply provided a place for people to relax—no pressure, no sales,
no questions asked. As I was preparing, I contacted Sally, one of
my mentors, to ask for her advice on how to train the people who
would be staffing the booth and providing a ministering presence to
the fairgoers.

Sally said, "First, I would teach about the importance of prayer—that
it's not about us but about Christ in us. Our responsibility is to stand

before him and soak in his presence. When we show up, we have no idea of the work he will do just because he is in us and we are there. Then just sit back and watch what happens in people's lives."

It's counterintuitive, isn't it? We live in a dying world, and we watch the hope drain from the faces of those around us. The condition of the human soul is an urgent one. The harvest is ripe and the workers are few. Since you're reading this book, you probably know all about that.

But the change doesn't start with an action plan or a ten–step process for reaching the lost—it all begins in the quiet. It begins with you, on your knees, seeking God, asking him to empower you, thanking him for his presence, and seeking his guidance.

How can you be sure that this is the right approach? Because God desires it. He wants you as close to him as possible. No effort to approach him is wasted; you can be sure he will honor a surrendered heart that clings to Him. A life of intimate prayer and worship is an impactful one.

You have nothing to offer apart from this important beginning, but everything to offer with it.

 ————————————————————————————————

PRESENCE PRACTICE

- In this chapter, we've suggested some parallels between the story of Gideon and our own journey of rethinking our role as evangelists. Read Gideon's full story in Judges 6–8. What other connections can you make between Gideon's lives and ours? What do you make of the Jubilee translation of Judges 6:34 ("And the Spirit of the LORD clothed himself in Gideon...")?

- The other key texts we've discussed in this chapter are Colossians 1:27 and Galatians 2:20. Study these two passages for yourself before moving on to the next chapter. How can they apply to you?

- It's not an accident that you picked up this book and encountered these passages from God's Word. What is the Spirit telling you through them?

 ——————————————————————————————————

Is Christ in you? We don't want to assume that the matter is settled just because you've picked up this book—but it can be. In Christ there is a great promise of freedom forever—freedom from fear, sin, pain, and death.

Your soul will live forever—and where you spend eternity is a matter of what you do on earth. If you've never committed your life to Jesus and asked him to live within you, it's simply a matter of inviting him. The three Scripture verses listed below provide the Biblical basis for the promise of salvation. They are followed by a prayer to guide you.

Right now, in this very moment, God is with you, calling you. The fact that you are reading these words is not a coincidence. He wants to do things in and through you that you could never guess, expect, or imagine—beautiful things. There is hope, and his name is Jesus Christ.

"If you declare that Jesus is Lord, and believe that God brought him back to life, you will be saved. By believing you receive God's approval, and by declaring your faith you are saved. Scripture says, 'Whoever believes in him will not be ashamed'" (Romans 10:9–11).

"However, when God our Savior made his kindness and love for humanity appear, he saved us, but not because of anything we had done to gain his approval. Instead, because of his mercy he saved us through the washing in which the Holy Spirit gives us new birth and renewal. God poured a generous amount of the Spirit on us through Jesus Christ our Savior. As a result, God in his kindness has given us his approval and we have become heirs who have the confidence that we have everlasting life" (Titus 3:4–7).

"Now you have been freed from sin and have become God's slaves. This results in a holy life and, finally, in everlasting life. The payment for sin is death, but the gift that God freely gives is everlasting life found in Christ Jesus our Lord" (Romans 6:22–23).

A Suggested Salvation Prayer

Father, I believe that Jesus is Lord—that he lived a sinless life on earth, was crucified on my behalf, and rose from the dead. I believe that I can have that same victory over death through him. I admit that I'm a sinner and that I need you. I am now committing my life to you, by your mercy and grace. I ask you to live in me as you promise; please ease my fears and forgive my sins. Thank you for hearing my prayer. In Christ's name I pray. Amen.

2
SHOWING UP

He's introduced as the traitor in the tree. Zacchaeus was first-century Jericho's chief tax collector, an astute accountant, and wealthy—someone who would be considered shady by today's standards. In the eyes of his fellow Jews, he was a sellout, a rat of the Roman government who turned his back on his people and squeezed them for more and more. In narrative terms, he was the stereotypical bad guy. But Zacchaeus was impacted by the power of presence—and it changed him forever.

When he heard Jesus was coming through Jericho, Zacchaeus was curious. He'd heard the news about the carpenter from Nazareth, and he wasn't going to pass up an opportunity to catch a glimpse of this prophet who some claimed could save souls, and who all acknowledged was making waves. Here is the biblical account:

> He tried to see who Jesus was. But Zacchaeus was a small man, and he couldn't see Jesus because of the crowd. So Zacchaeus ran ahead and climbed a fig tree to see Jesus, who was coming that way.
>
> When Jesus came to the tree, he looked up and said, "Zacchaeus, come down! I must stay at your house today."

Zacchaeus came down and was glad to welcome Jesus into his home. But the people who saw this began to express disapproval. They said, "He went to be the guest of a sinner."

Later, at dinner, Zacchaeus stood up and said to the Lord, "Lord, I'll give half of my property to the poor. I'll pay four times as much as I owe to those I have cheated in any way."

Then Jesus said to Zacchaeus, "You and your family have been saved today. You've shown that you, too, are one of Abraham's descendants."
(Luke 19:3–9)

As you read this familiar story, think about what we *don't* know. We know that Jesus had an odd encounter with an unpopular man who'd climbed a tree. We know that Jesus invited himself to the man's home and that the man and his family were saved. But we don't know what happened once Jesus walked through the door. We don't know what prompted the traitor in the tree to stand up in the middle of dinner and dramatically repent. We don't even know what Jesus said during his visit. In the account, as soon as Jesus decides to pay Zacchaeus a visit, Luke shifts the focus to people's disapproval of Jesus and his questionable decision to dine with a deceiver. That shifts says a lot about what the Lord wants us to see in this story.

What we do know is that the Lord did something very simple, something anyone can do—he visited. Could he have saved Zacchaeus while Zacchaeus was clutching to a tree branch like a stray cat? Of course he could have. But Jesus decided to do something more in this interaction, for Zacchaeus and for us. The Lord wanted to spend time with him, to share a meal and conversation. The result? Repentance and salvation for an entire family. Because Jesus chose to *be there* for Zacchaeus, his life was eternally changed. That's the heart of presence.

Zacchaeus's repentance wasn't the result of an altar call, or even a challenge from Jesus specifically. It was a response to the powerful presence of Jesus. It's no accident that the story of Zacchaeus concludes with Jesus's mission statement for his earthly ministry. After what happened to Zacchaeus, Jesus provides a moral for the story, a takeaway from the encounter: "Indeed, the Son of Man has come to seek and to save people who are lost" (Luke 19:10). It's a truth that's had a historical impact—from that tree in first-century Jericho, to the walls of your home today.

The Son of Man has come to *seek and to save*. If you are a believer, you may have thought quite a bit about that second verb, *save*. You are likely quite aware of and grateful for your salvation. You may think of your own soul when you read such texts as Ephesians 2:1: "You were once dead because of your failures and sins." But as verse 5 reminds us, God "made us alive together with Christ" (2:5). And so, you have been saved from death.

But have you considered the first verb in the pair—that you were also *sought*? Before you were saved, you were on his mind, in his eye. He directed others, aligned circumstances, pursued you. He set his sights on rescuing you from a life of sin and death.

I (Margaret) remember driving down the road from our house one Saturday morning more than 20 years ago. For some reason, the parable of the sower was on my mind (you'll find the text in full at the end of this chapter.) It had been years since I had heard the parable, but it was strange that I would recall it at that moment—I wasn't following the Lord and had no interest in doing so. I was raised in a Christian home and had heard countless Bible stories repeated over and over; I knew what the Bible said. Still, in that moment, there was no logical reason why I would have been thinking of that parable, or any parable for that matter. Really, I couldn't have cared less.

But, strangely, as the story formed in my mind, I began to lay it like a grid over my life. In a moment, I realized that I was the stony ground from the story—that any God-borne seed that might fall on me would just land on the dormant rocks of my heart and be snatched away. I was as dry and dead as dust.

As I considered what that meant—what it really meant—my stomach sank and tears gathered. In my heart, in that moment, I knew. In fact, I think I said out loud in the car, "I don't want to be stony ground! I want to be fertile soil!" I knew my life had to be different. I knew I should start going to church.

That's when I remembered three of my clients at the hair salon where I worked. All three were from the same church, and each one had been patiently and persistently inviting me to their church, Harrisonburg (Virginia) First Church of the Nazarene. They didn't give up on me, and God was seeking me. I went the following Sunday, and I've been part of that congregation ever since. And now I'm on our pastoral team and co-writing a book about presence evangelism! God pursued me, and his people were agents of his restoration of my life. They didn't have special training or particularly charismatic personalities. They were simply *there*. Present. And God can do the same through you for the ones you love. The Son of Man continues to seek and to save.

Have you ever needed someone to just be there for you? Can you remember times in your life when you were hurting or lonely? You weren't interested in advice or in seven steps to a better life. You just wanted to know that you weren't alone—that there was comfort and hope in the presence of another person.

The question this book asks is simple: Are you willing to be there for others? To be present? If you're willing, God will use you. You don't need special skills, gifts, or a particular personality type. In fact, as Jesus-believers filled with his holy presence, we too often underestimate the power of simply showing up for others. All you need to do is what Jesus did—be there.

A well-known movie director once said, "Showing up is 80 percent of life." In many ways, that's what this book is about—the wonderful and powerful practice of showing up, of being present for another person. In the past, when it came to Christians relating to non-Christians, this was known as "friendship evangelism" or "relationship evangelism." We're using the term "presence" because we believe it's the most important aspect of influencing others, especially those who don't yet know Christ. It starts with Christ's presence in you, as we discussed in Chapter 1, and is fulfilled when that same presence of Christ works in others through you. This, in turn, requires you to be present in others' lives. That's why we define presence evangelism as a lifestyle of manifesting Christ *in* you to those *around* you.

Before you can do or say anything, you must be present, ready to connect, and ready to care—no strings attached. This means patiently offering a hand of friendship to anyone and everyone who will accept it. In the end, presence is not about getting people to do what we want them to do but doing what God calls us to do.

That's the nature of presence as we define it. It starts with a meaningful connection with another person—an agenda-free openness to building a relationship. And that connection has a single objective: to care. Sounds almost too simple, doesn't it? Yet that's what we see in Jesus's interaction with Zacchaeus.

I (Kerry) traveled to Germany a few years back to speak at an evangelistic outreach in the city of Mainz. Each morning, I trained the staff before the evening services. For one of the sessions, my lesson was about presence. Specifically, I was teaching that we don't always give enough credit to the power of simply showing up. We think we always have to create this complex plan and strategy for whatever we're doing, wherever we're going. We stress and strain, believing that we're doing noble work. And we are, but there is great power in simply *being there*. Sometimes plans can actually bog us down. So I told the workers, "Just make sure Christ lives in you, then go into the world, and he will work!"

One of the young pastors, Cris, was my interpreter that morning. As I spoke, I noticed that he looked more and more anxious, but I didn't know why. I thought something I said must have really been bothering him. After the session, I asked him what was on his mind.

"I honestly don't know if I believe what you were teaching this morning," he said. "It sounds too simple. Too easy."

That night we were preparing for the service. About an hour before it started, Cris approached me with a strange look on his face. He asked if we could talk privately. So we found a bench near the river that flowed past the outdoor meeting place.

"Kerry, I need to apologize to you," he said. "I told you I was skeptical of the presence ministry you were talking about this morning. So after I finished interpreting for you, I went to a coffee shop and sat down and dared God to prove that it was right. Frankly, I doubted it was."

At this point, I began to smile. I suspected what was coming because I'd heard similar stories. It's so easy to doubt the power of presence. You may have even felt a little skeptical reading this.

Cris continued, "But all afternoon in that little coffee shop, people came to me wanting to talk about spiritual things. The truth is, I went in with a Jonah-like spirit. I didn't even want it to work. But it did—over and over. One man who talked to me is coming to the meeting tonight. I believe he's given his life to Christ—all because I did something as simple as taking a seat in a coffee shop. Just because I was present! It's truly humbling and amazing."

Can you do that? Can you sit
and talk? Can you let Jesus in
you come through in a way that
is comfortable and natural?

Now, whenever I go back to Germany, Cris introduces me by saying, "This is the pastor who taught me my ministry philosophy: the philosophy of presence!"

Once again, it's important to understand that when we use the word "presence" as the basis for this book, we're not talking about your skill. We're not talking about you becoming a master Bible teacher, theologian, or learned scholar of the ancient texts who can persuade anyone with your impressive intellect and wit. We're not talking about you becoming a charismatic figure who captures a room just by entering it. We're not talking about you becoming an expert salesperson who makes the close on soul after soul before moving on to the next conquest. We're not really talking about you at all, but Christ *in* you.

Of course, knowing your Bible, relating to others, and winning souls are imperatives for the Christian life—we are not minimizing any of those responsibilities. But those things are not the primary focus of the term "presence." Rather, if you've ever been a friend; if you've ever visited someone; if you've ever cared for someone—you are ready to practice presence evangelism.

In the April 30, 2014, issue of *Catholic Stand*, Melanie Jean Juneau tells a story that captures the nature of presence evangelism:

> Three years ago I was stranded for ten hours in an airport with an East German archaeologist. He spoke of his work, and I shared funny stories about living with nine kids. I did not preach.
>
> Suddenly he asked, "What is it about you? You are the most powerful person I have ever met."
>
> His statement shocked me. Sure, I felt God and his joy bubbling up within me, but I had not prayed for or healed this man. I'd simply made him laugh. Yet, somehow, even though he was an atheist, we were both aware of a power flowing around us! It was tangible.

This is *presence evangelism*. God does all the work—we simply relax and watch. There's no room for ego or pride because it's all about God, not us.

Earlier, we mentioned The Resting Place, our church's outreach at our annual county fair. To create The Resting Place, we set up in an area along a heavily trafficked pathway and fill it with rocking chairs. We don't sell anything, and we really don't even promote the church. Our only goal is to provide a place where hustled and bustled fairgoers can relax and enjoy their funnel cake. For us, it's a wonderful opportunity to just be with people. It's our way of ministering presence.

One evening, I (Kerry) noticed that a lady sitting in one of the corner chairs was watching us. For a few hours, she observed as we greeted folks and invited them to stay awhile. I noticed her a couple of times, but just left her alone. That's the beauty of the idea—we engage people, but only when they're ready.

As the end of the evening neared, the lady finally called me over. As I approached, the first words out of her mouth were, "You can't fool me!" At first, I wasn't sure what she meant. By the tone of her voice it was almost as if she was accusing me of something. But then I chuckled when she gestured toward the other people at our booth. "You can't fool me. I know what you're doing here. You're hosting the presence of Jesus at the county fair." Precisely!

Can you do that? Can you sit and talk? Can you let Jesus in you come through in a way that is comfortable and natural? Can you listen? Can you be there? You'd be amazed at what the Spirit can do through a willing vessel.

PRESENCE PRACTICE #1

The people around you are not in your life by accident. If you are in Christ and have an obedient heart, the Lord has given you friends, relatives, coworkers and acquaintances who do not yet know him. This book was really written for those precious souls.

There are seven blank spaces below; think about five people you're close to who, as far as you can determine, do not know Christ. Write their names in five of the spaces.

Leave the remaining two spaces blank. Those spaces are for the names of the people you'll be able to influence because you're reading this book. It's amazing how the Lord honors those who commit to a life of presence. Because you have a heart to connect and care, we believe he has more in store for you than you can imagine.

1. _My son Bill_
2. _Jim Pryor_
3. _____
4. _____
5. _____
6. _____
7. _____

Next, duplicate the list on a separate piece of paper and post it somewhere you'll see it every day. Determine to do something to make yourself present to each of the five people you've listed over the next thirty days. This is not a call to preach or even to invite people to church. If presence can be considered an ongoing conversation, this is a call to start the dialogue—to connect and care.

To complete the two blank spaces, all you have to do is pay attention. As you pray and seek a life of presence, the Lord will bring people-opportunities to you. When he does, write the names of the first two people in those blank spaces. You don't have to wonder whether they will present themselves—they will.

PRESENCE PRACTICE #2

Read Luke 15 and Luke 19:10, then consider the following questions:

- Why is the lost becoming found so important in heaven?

- There will be more happiness in heaven over one person who turns to God than over ninety-nine people who already have God's approval (15:7). Why does Jesus emphasize that point?

- Can you identify the moment God found you? What were the most important events that led to that moment? Who influenced you? How?

- What do the sheep, the coin, the son, and Zacchaeus have in common? They were all lost but then was found

❖ ❖ ❖

Read the parable of the sower below (from Margaret's story earlier in the chapter):

That same day Jesus left the house and sat down by the Sea of Galilee. The crowd that gathered around him was so large that he got into a boat. He sat in the boat while the entire crowd stood on the shore. Then he used stories as illustrations to tell them many things.

He said, "Listen! A farmer went to plant seed. Some seeds were planted along the road, and birds came and devoured them. Other seeds were planted on rocky ground, where there was little soil. The plants sprouted quickly because the soil wasn't deep. But when the sun came up, they were scorched. They withered because their roots weren't deep enough. Other seeds were planted among thornbushes, and the thornbushes grew up and choked them. But other seeds were planted on good ground and produced grain. They produced one hun-

dred, sixty, or thirty times as much as was planted. Let the person who has ears listen!"
(Matthew 13:1–9)

What kind of soil do you think you are? What support would you offer for your answer?

3
OLD THINGS

❖

The Bible may be an ancient text, but it pushes us to new horizons—new approaches, new ideas, and new ways of thinking. God's Word won't let us get bogged down in the past—in our old ways of life. It transforms us.

> Therefore, I urge you, brothers and sisters, in view of God's mercy, to offer your bodies as a living sacrifice, holy and pleasing to God—this is your true and proper worship. Do not conform to the pattern of this world, but be transformed by the renewing of your mind. Then you will be able to test and approve what God's will is—his good, pleasing and perfect will. (Romans 12:1–2, NIV)

> Therefore, if anyone is in Christ, the new creation has come: The old has gone, the new is here! All this is from God, who reconciled us to himself through Christ and gave us the ministry of reconciliation: that God was reconciling the world to himself in Christ, not counting people's sins against them. And he has committed to us the message of reconciliation. (2 Corinthians 5:17–19, NIV)

Fruitfulness in presence evangelism depends on your willingness to think differently, to renew your mind so that having the mind of

Christ (see 1 Corinthians 2:16) isn't just a theological concept, but informs the way you view your purpose on earth and God's purposes for those who don't know him.

Presence evangelism isn't a new idea—just look at the story of Zacchaeus. We didn't write this book to introduce a brand new concept. Instead, we want to suggest that, in a culture that is desperate for connection (and continually invents new technologies in search of it), going back to the ministry of presence might be the best way to fulfill the Great Commission.

Perhaps if the old ways haven't been working for you, you're ready to try something new.

Not many people talk about Billy Sunday anymore. But at one time, he was the face of evangelism in America—Billy Sunday was Billy Graham before Billy Graham.

Sunday didn't start as one of America's first great evangelists; rather, he started as one of America's first great baseball players. He made a name for himself in 1883, after signing a Chicago White Stockings contract with the man who some consider the inventor of baseball—Albert Goodwill Spalding. Billy Sunday became a baseball pioneer—a superstar before there were superstars.

But in 1886, something happened to Sunday. A missions team from a local church was preaching and singing hymns on a Chicago street corner. There, Sarah "Ma" Clarke of the Pacific Garden Mission led Sunday to the Lord. He committed his life to Christ, eventually ending his baseball career and forever changing his life and the lives of thousands of others. Billy Sunday would go from ballplayer to preacher, the first media evangelist in American history.

By the turn of the twentieth century, Sunday's name was synonymous with evangelism. He preached to thousands in revival meetings across the country, with hundreds being saved at every stop.

He was bold, passionate, and eloquent. Sunday preached a clear and uncompromising gospel, and virtually pioneered large-scale "event evangelism" in concert halls and arenas. In his famous 1917 New York campaign, 98,000 people accepted Christ over ten weeks of meetings. The country had never seen anything like it.

Almost exactly a year after Billy Sunday's famous New York campaign, William Franklin Graham, Jr., was born on a dairy farm near Charlotte, North Carolina. You probably know Billy Graham's story—he followed Sunday's lead and became the most impactful evangelist in history. It's estimated that he preached the gospel to 215 million people in 185 countries—and that doesn't count those he reached by television and radio. Many consider the Billy Graham evangelistic model to be the gold standard: he used tent-revival-type promotion to gather thousands of people in an arena, then focused on music, a clear presentation of the gospel, and a specific invitation to repentance. Counselors were available to lead people to Christ and help them find a church home. It's an evangelism model that worked gloriously.

In 1962, Dr. D. James Kennedy, senior pastor of Coral Ridge Presbyterian Church in Fort Lauderdale, Florida, developed a program partly based on Billy Graham's model called Evangelism Explosion (EE), which provides a specific set of guidelines and scripts for leading someone to Christ. It is the most popular evangelism guide ever produced and has been translated into seventy languages; it is estimated that twenty thousand churches have used EE.

Evangelism Explosion's approach to outreach has been called confrontational evangelism because it challenges the unsaved to consider and respond to their fallen state. The EE process is based on two diagnostic questions to help a lost person evaluate their spiritual health. The first question is, "Do you know for sure that you are going to be with God in heaven?" The second is, "If God were to ask you, 'Why should I let you into my heaven?' what would you say?" The answers to these questions often facilitate conversations about the gospel, which can in turn lead to people committing their lives to Christ.

In the past, EE has often been used in cold-call contexts, in which individuals or teams walk through neighborhoods or set up a station in a public place in hopes of facilitating an intentional encounter with someone. Throughout the years, the Lord has undoubtedly used the EE model to reach many.

Billy Sunday, Billy Graham, and Evangelism Explosion represent different approaches to evangelism. The Billy Sunday/Billy Graham model relies on the power of a forceful, charismatic preacher who is faithful to the biblical text and elicits a swift response from his or her hearers; Evangelism Explosion equips all types of church members for witnessing by teaching them strategies for engaging the unsaved.

Before we look at the challenges that these well-known evangelism models may present, we want to be clear: if it leads to a lost person finding Christ, there is no such thing as bad evangelism. Remember, "the Son of Man came to seek and to save the lost" (Luke 19:10). Anything God can use to win more people for heaven is a good thing, so whenever a person created in the image of God comes to salvation, it is a cause for celebration. In fact, Jesus tells us it is the most joyous thing in the world: "I tell you that in the same way there will be more rejoicing in heaven over one sinner who repents than over ninety-nine righteous persons who do not need to repent" (Luke 15:7, NIV). As believers, our fundamental purpose is to manifest Jesus—to be his witnesses wherever we go. There is still a place for stadium campaigns and door-to-door efforts—we're not suggesting that presence evangelism should replace other evange- lism strategies. Rather, we've based this book on one simple truth: *every* believer can be active in fulfilling the Great Commission. Every believer can obey Christ by loving others and caring about the state of their souls. Every Christian is called to "do the work of an evangelist" (2 Timothy 4:5b, NIV).

Not everyone can be a Billy Sunday or a Billy Graham. Not everyone can witness door to door with a memorized script. The intimidating prospect of buttonholing strangers into making a decision for Christ has caused some believers to assume that evangelism simply isn't for them. As a result, many resign and move to the sidelines, content to let pastors do all the outreach—and that's the problem that motivated the writing of this book.

The truth is, no matter your personality, talent, or spiritual gifting, you *can* influence others. And if you can influence others, you can play a role in what God wants to do in their lives. That leads us back to the most powerful way you can impact another person: presence.

In its March 3, 1997, issue, *Christianity Today* published a feature titled "Outreach: Evangelism Explosion Retools Its Approach." Part of this article read:

> Evangelism Explosion (EE), one of the world's most widely used methods of church-based outreach, is changing its approach to emphasize relationship-building and discipling new believers. . . .
>
> Too confrontational? Results of an EE-commissioned study released in January showed that more than half of those churches not using EE called the method "confrontational evangelism." Many of these pastors cited doubts about EE's "relevancy to meet the needs of today's people" and a perception that EE was "weak" relationally.
>
> "The questions people are asking today are very different," acknowledges EE executive vice president Tom Stebbins. "Even the objections they are raising are different. Back then it was, *Is the Bible true?* Today it's, *Is there a God after all? Is there really life after death?*"

When the EE leadership team realized that the old model for evangelism wasn't as effective in 1997 as it had been in 1977, they determined to make changes: they shifted the emphasis from cold

Once again, presence
evangelism isn't a new concept.
It's not something we invented.
We're simply suggesting that it
fits the needs of the
twenty-first century—
and in that way,
it fits with God's purposes.

calls and quick decisions to relationship-building and discipleship. They recognized that, while the gospel message doesn't change, approaches to its delivery may.

Now, more than twenty years later, we're suggesting the presence evangelism approach can be a powerful tool for reaching the lost. God's message of hope hasn't changed, but our world has; we are living in a time of unprecedented technological growth, and people are increasingly hurt by the ravages of sin.

This is why we're calling for an approach that emphasizes not *doing* so much as *being*—because we believe that if we are faithful to show up in people's lives, God will be faithful to show his presence and power through us. When it comes to presence, ability is less crucial than *availability*.

Once again, presence evangelism isn't a new concept. It's not something we invented. We're simply suggesting that it fits the needs of the twenty-first century—and in that way, it fits with God's purposes. It fits with a generation of lost neighbors; it fits with believers who truly want to make a difference in the world around them.

If the word *presence* is throwing you off or seems too abstract, think about the word *friendship*. You have good friends; you *are* a good friend. If someone asked you to describe friendship, you could immediately come up with descriptive words: loyalty, care, faithfulness, forgiveness, comfort, fun, and so on.

Presence evangelism asks this question: What if we simply became good friends with the people in our circles who don't know Christ? Trusted friends; no-strings-attached friends. Friends who build relationships by listening. Friends who sacrifice. You can think of times when you were a true friend to someone—but it might be easier to think of times when someone was a true friend to *you*.

Judith Heicksen recounts in an issue of *Reader's Digest* a memorable encounter with presence evangelism:

Five months after my husband, my two-year-old daughter, and I moved two thousand miles from home, I gave birth to a beautiful baby girl with severely clubbed feet. This marked the beginning of a long series of doctor appointments. Taking care of two young children, one of whom required constant medical attention, meant that I was always tired and behind on my household chores. One day, we came home from yet another doctor's visit to find the front door ajar. I cautiously proceeded into the house, only to find the floors spotless, the dishes cleaned and dried, and the dirty laundry washed and folded. Upstairs, the beds were made, and there were even flowers in a vase beside my bed. It turns out that my friend Joy was driving by my home and noticed my car was gone, so she took the opportunity to help me out. I learned an important lesson that day about compassion. And this friendship was sealed for life!

Author Anne Lamott calls friendship a holy connection. "Friendship" is a feeble word for an extraordinary and holy connection—for what can be the most sustaining, life-giving, death-defying relationships some of us will ever experience. My closest friends are the reason for my deep faith in God—it's through them that I've discovered what superhuman intimacy and devotion look like. I have been blessed by people whose unconditional love and loyalty have helped me survive.

Presence evangelism is not a complicated concept. It doesn't require special skills. If you're concerned that this book is calling you to become something you're not, or perfect all your weaknesses, we can put your mind at ease: if you can be a friend, you can do this. If you *need* a friend, you have what it takes to begin this journey.

In the *Catholic Stand* article "Presence Evangelism," Melanie Jean Juneau writes:

The stars have fallen. The big names have grown old. Society is weary of huge, dazzling Christian shows. People crave reality. They do not respond to the evangelism of the 20th century. Of course God is working through new technology as well, but he is also using his little ones in a new way.

Evangelism has gone through many stages to reach the place we are today. Up until the late sixties, evangelists were mainly preachers of the Word. . . .

The primary way the Holy Spirit touched people in large crowds in the seventies, eighties, and nineties was through power evangelism. Rather than preaching long sermons, the evangelists who drew the largest crowds were prophets and healers. The Spirit fell in a tangible way. . . .

Now the Spirit of God is moving among the grassroots. It is an entirely different kind of evangelism . . . It is time for the little people to shine.

PRESENCE PRACTICE

Read Acts 1:8 and 2 Corinthians 5:16–19, then answer the questions that follow.

But you will receive power when the Holy Spirit comes to you. Then you will be my witnesses to testify about me in Jerusalem, throughout Judea and Samaria, and to the ends of the earth. (Acts 1:8)

So from now on we don't think of anyone from a human point of view. If we did think of Christ from a human point of view, we don't anymore. Whoever is a believer in Christ is a new creation. The old way of living has disappeared. A new way of living has come into existence. God has done all this. He has restored our relationship with him through Christ, and has given us this ministry of restoring relationships. In other words, God was using Christ to restore his relationship with humanity. He didn't hold people's faults against them, and he has given us this message of restored relationships to tell others. (2 Corinthians 5:16–19)

In both of these texts, something important happens *before* Christians respond. Something happens *before* we become witnesses, and *before* we enter the ministry of restoring relationships. Paul's statements in the 2 Corinthians text make it clear that we are only able to share "this message of restored relationships" (verse 18) because God "has restored our relationship with him through Christ" (verse 19).

- What is your role in communicating the message of restored relationships?

- What might the "message of restored relationships" sound like in your own words?

- What's the connection between presence, friendship and restored relationships?

4
PRESENCE TODAY

Whose Esther are you?

Queen Esther is, of course, one of the shining biblical models of faithfulness, courage, and heroism. God used Esther to save his people from the first recorded attempted genocide in world history. Esther stood in the gap for others—an idea that is really the heartbeat of this book. As we study her story more closely, we find a verse that teaches us the importance of a commitment to presence evangelism.

Esther lived about 450 years before the birth of Christ, in Persia (the area we now know as Iran). At that time, Jews were scattered throughout the known world, and Esther and her guardian Mordecai were part of the faithful group in the capital city of Susa, where Persian King Xerxes "ruled over 127 provinces from India to Sudan" (Esther 1:1). Before he knew she was a Jew, King Xerxes deposed the former Queen Vashti and chose Esther as his new queen.

One of Xerxes's political advisors was Haman, the antagonist of the story. When Mordecai would not bow down to him, Haman grew angry and persuaded the king to declare a genocide against the Jews. To say that the stakes in this story are high would be an understatement.

Mordecai sent word to Esther, begging her to use her position as queen to appeal to the king on her people's behalf. Here is the Biblical account:

> So Hathak went out to Mordecai in the open square of the city in front of the king's gate. Mordecai told him everything that had happened to him, including the exact amount of money Haman had promised to pay into the royal treasury for the destruction of the Jews. He also gave him a copy of the text of the edict for their annihilation, which had been published in Susa, to show to Esther and explain it to her, and he told him to instruct her to go into the king's presence to beg for mercy and plead with him for her people.
>
> Hathak went back and reported to Esther what Mordecai had said. Then she instructed him to say to Mordecai, "All the king's officials and the people of the royal provinces know that for any man or woman who approaches the king in the inner court without being summoned the king has but one law: that they be put to death unless the king extends the gold scepter to them and spares their lives. But thirty days have passed since I was called to go to the king."
>
> When Esther's words were reported to Mordecai, he sent back this answer: "Do not think that because you are in the king's house you alone of all the Jews will escape."
> (Esther 4:6–13, NIV)

When Mordecai first urged her to approach King Xerxes, Esther hesitated. She understood the danger of approaching the king uninvited, and of exposing herself as a Jew. She knew she could easily lose her life in the process. But Mordecai's response to her hesitation seems to have emboldened Esther. This is the verse we mentioned—the one that sheds light on our passion for presence evangelism. In Esther 4:14, Mordecai essentially tells Esther, "The fact is, even if you remain silent now, someone else will help rescue the Jews, but you and your relatives will die. And who knows, you may have gained your royal position for such a time as this."

"For such a time as this." If Mordecai were alive today, perhaps he would have worded it like this: "Maybe you are who you are and *where* you are because God has a specific purpose for you—a purpose beyond yourself. A call to save others. Will you step forward?"

Will you? Whether you have days or decades left, what is the difference you can make with your life? How can you, like Esther, leave a legacy that will never be extinguished?

There was nothing ordinary about Esther's world—politically and culturally, it was a unique time in history. It was a time with a Jewish queen in a region where Jews were in exile, and it was the first recorded instance of genocide. When Mordecai referred to "such a time as this," he wasn't speaking in abstract terms; he fully believed that God had positioned Esther to make a difference in that unique moment in history.

The same is true for you—we too are living in circumstances that have no precedent in the past and won't be replicated in the future. You too are positioned to serve God and others in "such a time as this." And we believe that presence evangelism is an important tool for reaching lost people in our time. In our time of unprecedented turmoil and technology, Jesus is actively reaching out to people where they are. Remember, he *pursues*.

Most of the Jews who were condemned to death by Haman's edict never knew they were on the verge of catastrophe. While others were unaware, Mordecai and Esther's faithfulness changed the course of history so that instead of being overcome, God's people were the overcomers (Esther 8:1–11).

In an analogy to your own life, you might say that you are Esther, and your friends and loved ones who don't know Christ are the people in mortal danger. Yet they're probably not aware of their peril—the most recent research indicates that most people believe that as long as they are "good people" and "do good things," they will *earn* heaven.

Part of what makes the twenty-first century unique is the way people view Christians and Christianity. The most recent demographic research indicates that attitudes toward the church and toward Christians are becoming increasingly hostile. For instance, data from the Barna Group, a research company, suggests that only 34 percent of "outsiders" believe that Christians truly care for them, while 64 percent of believers think that non-Christians perceive Christians as sincere (for more information, watch "What If Starbucks Marketed Like a Church? A Parable," available on YouTube).

In one book for "such a time as this," titled *unChristian: What a New Generation Really Thinks about Christianity . . . and Why It Matters*, authors David Kinnaman and Gabe Lyons present some of the latest research about nonbelievers' perspectives on faith, religion, Christianity, and Christians: "Christianity has become bloated with blind followers who would rather repeat slogans than actually feel true compassion and care. Christianity has become marketed and streamlined into a juggernaut of fear mongering that has lost its own heart." Later, the authors add: "Among young outsiders . . . 84 percent say they personally know at least one committed Christian. Yet just 15 percent thought the lifestyles of those Christ followers were significantly different from the norm. This gap speaks volumes."

On top of that, many who don't know Christ believe that Christians view them as just another "notch on their belt"—just a project to check off a list, someone to be coerced into the kingdom of God. An example of this perception is found in twenty-two-year-old Shawn's response to one of the Barna surveys: "Christians are too concerned with converting people. They are insincere. All I ever hear is 'Get saved!' I tried that whole Jesus thing already. It didn't work for me before, and I am not interested now."

Meanwhile, people are
also craving meaning and
connection. We're developing
new communication
technologies fast enough to
make our heads spin, yet with
all these desperate attempts
to feel connected, we are more
isolated than ever.

Kinnaman and Lyons go on to further explain the gap between why Christians *think* outsiders reject Christianity, and the *actual* reasons why they do:

> Our research shows that Christians believe the primary reason outsiders have rejected Christ is that they cannot handle the rigorous standards of following Christ. There is a nuance here that allows Christians to feel like they're better than other people, more capable of being holy and sinless. We rationalize that outsiders don't want to become Christ followers because they can't really cut it.
>
> The truth is that few outsiders say they avoid Christianity because the moral standards are too restrictive. Only one-quarter of young outsiders are convinced Christianity would limit their lifestyle and options in life. Instead, outsiders said they have never become a Christ follower for a number of other reasons: because they have never thought about it, because they are not particularly interested in spirituality, because they are already committed to another faith, or because they are repelled by Christians.

Researcher and consultant Thom Rainer further adds to this conversation: he led a study to determine what percentage of Americans 1) identify as Christians and 2) understand that being a Christian means putting your faith for salvation in Christ alone. Rainer found that among Americans born before 1946, 65 percent identified themselves as Christians and were able to articulate the basics of the gospel. For those born between 1946 and 1964, the number dropped to 35 percent. For those born between 1965 and 1976, it fell to a scant 15 percent. Finally, among Americans born between 1974 and 1994, only 4 percent of the population identified themselves as Christians and said they trusted Christ alone for their salvation.

With those findings in mind, here are some of the things that characterize our time:

- People don't know (or care) about the gospel. They see "salvation" as a matter of being good, if they accept the concept of salvation at all.

- Unbelievers don't believe that Christians really care about them. They think believers are just looking for another notch in their evangelistic belt.

- Unbelievers perceive essentially no difference when comparing the lifestyles of Christians and the lifestyles of non-Christians.

- Whether it's justified or not, unbelievers have a generally negative perception of believers. They perceive Christians as generally shallow, hypocritical, condemning, or all of the above.

- A very low percentage of adults (especially adults under the age of 40) are truly committed disciples of Jesus Christ. While the percentage of Americans who say they believe in God remains well over 50%, fewer and fewer appear to reflect this belief in their lifestyle.

Meanwhile, people are also craving meaning and connection. We're developing new communication technologies fast enough to make our heads spin, yet with all these desperate attempts to feel connected, we are more isolated than ever. The March 30, 2015, issue of *The Independent* featured a headline that asked an important question: "The loneliness epidemic: We're more connected than ever—but are we feeling more alone?" Their answer was a resounding yes. They wrote:

> So why are we getting lonelier? Changes in modern society are considered to be the cause. We live in nuclear family units, often living large distances away from our extended family and friends, and our growing reliance on social technology rather than face to face interaction is thought to be making us feel more isolated. It means we feel less connected to others

and our relationships are becoming more superficial and less rewarding.

We are social animals and need to feel that we "belong" to others and feel connected to one another. Social pain is as real a sensation for us as physical pain; researchers have shown that loneliness and rejection activates the same parts of the brain as physical pain.

By now it should be clear why we believe that God calls Christians to presence evangelism. There are two fundamental principles that drive this idea:

1. Now more than ever, "Christians" *must* be true believers. There can be no more credence given to the idea of a "nominal Christian." If you consider yourself a disciple of Jesus Christ, you must live as a disciple. Presence evangelism starts with loving Jesus passionately and without compromise. It starts with his taking up residence in you and wearing you like a garment, as we discussed in Chapter 1. If you want what God wants, you're on your way.

2. The presence evangelist gives up life in the comfort zone to build meaningful, no-strings-attached relationships with others, especially those who don't yet know Christ. When you're in God's sweet spot, you don't need to be needed, but desire to be available. These relationships are based on true connection and unconditional care. That means you listen, laugh, and love in an atmosphere of loyalty. And when the time comes to share Christ, you are ready—not with a sales pitch, but with a personal testimony of his faithfulness. Then you leave the rest to him.

There is an important caveat to the no-strings-attached attitude toward friendship that we've referenced here. The idea is that you enter in your presence-based relationships without placing expectations or requirements on your friend. It means extending God's love without expecting anything in return; pursuing the relationship not to get, but to give. It means staying by someone's side even when the results aren't what you expected.

However, "no strings attached" won't necessarily apply to the other person in the relationship. In fact, you may need to be prepared for several strings. The other person may place expectations on you—expectations of loyalty, reliability, and trustworthiness. Be prepared to be needed, to be depended upon. Please note that we are not advocating relationships without wise boundaries. These relationships should be free of manipulation, codependence and fear—but that doesn't mean they will be free of work.

Ultimately, the presence evangelist has an effect on people. If you're doing it right, you will matter to others—people will seek your presence. However, if your presence doesn't make an impact, your absence won't make a difference.

I (Kerry) had a favorite local restaurant called China Jade that was run by a precious couple named Annie and Jackie Ling. For about fifteen years I frequented their restaurant on a regular basis. Yes, I loved the food, but it was more than that—I felt almost a sense of call to that little place in an insignificant strip mall. Over time, the Lings and I became such friends that we even exchanged gifts at Christmas!

At one point a few years back, I went on sabbatical for about eight weeks. When I returned, one of my first stops was China Jade. As the waiter seated me, he didn't offer me a menu or take my order. Instead he said, "You wait here—Annie wants to talk to you!"

I watched him walk through the swinging kitchen doors. A moment later, Annie burst out of the kitchen with tears in her eyes and rushed toward me. I had no idea what was going on, but I braced myself to be thrown out of my favorite restaurant!

Annie started talking before she even got to my table. "I thought you had died! I missed you! Don't ever leave town for more than two weeks without telling me!"

Sure, Annie had missed me on some level. We liked each other. We were friends. But it was more than that. She cried because she missed the presence of Jesus coming into her restaurant and loving her with no strings attached. I loved allowing Christ to make meaningful connection with the Lings through me. I didn't stand on the table and preach. I didn't make sure my Bible was conspicuous each time I visited. I was just *there* for them.

The Lings have since moved back to China, so staying in touch has been difficult. Nevertheless, I truly believe we will see each other in heaven someday. (And I hope they have a hand in preparing the marriage supper of the Lamb. Trust me, you'll love it!)

PRESENCE PRACTICE

- When Mordecai asked Esther to act on her people's behalf, how did she respond and why? (See 4:4–11.) What might that teach us about committing to presence evangelism?

- Why do you think Esther ultimately decided to put her life on the line for her peoples' sake? (See 4:12–17.)

In this chapter, you read the following quote from David Kinnaman and Gabe Lyons: "Christianity has become bloated with blind followers who would rather repeat slogans than actually feel true compassion and care. Christianity has become marketed and streamlined into a juggernaut of fear mongering that has lost its own heart."

- Do you agree? Why or why not?

- What can you do specifically to change this perception within your sphere of influence?

Read John 15:13–16 and Philippians 2:3–8:

The greatest love you can show is to give your life for your friends. You are my friends if you obey my commandments. I don't call you servants anymore, because a servant doesn't know what his master is doing. But I've called you friends

because I've made known to you everything that I've heard from my Father. You didn't choose me, but I chose you. I have appointed you to go, to produce fruit that will last, and to ask the Father in my name to give you whatever you ask for.
(John 15:13–16)

Don't act out of selfish ambition or be conceited. Instead, humbly think of others as being better than yourselves. Don't be concerned only about your own interests, but also be concerned about the interests of others. Have the same attitude that Christ Jesus had. Although he was in the form of God and equal with God, he did not take advantage of this equality. Instead, he emptied himself by taking on the form of a servant, by becoming like other humans, by having a human appearance. He humbled himself by becoming obedient to the point of death, death on a cross.
(Philippians 2:3–8)

- Based on what you've read so far, how do you interpret these two texts in the light of presence evangelism?

- What do you think the unbelievers in your life want or need from you?

5
THE HOME FIRES

This chapter is about home base—not in the baseball sense, but in terms of the foundation for presence evangelism. We see that foundation in two areas.

First, a commitment to presence evangelism starts at home—literally. If home is where the heart is, it's also where a life of presence must begin. It's where you learn the art of welcoming God's presence into your life and encouraging your family members to do the same. It's where you practice being present. Your home should be a place where everyone seeks God while graciously and generously giving their presence to each other.

Secondly, we have identified five promises that serve as a foundation for all the ideas we write about here. These promises serve as a launching point for the lifestyle of presence. They are the home fires for a life committed to the ideas in this book.

Written more than one hundred years ago during World War I, the British song "Keep the Home Fires Burning," by Ivor Novello and Lena Guilbert Ford, expresses the importance of the home. We believe its message speaks to the notion of the home as a presence-evangelism sanctuary. The song's lyrics include the following words:

> They were summoned from the hillside,
> They were called in from the glen,
> And the country found them ready
> At the stirring call for men
> Let no tears add to their hardships
> As the soldiers pass along,
> And although your heart is breaking,
> Make it sing this cheery song:
> Keep the home fires burning,
> While your hearts are yearning.
> Though your lads are far away
> They dream of home.

No matter where you call home, that place is the anchor point for presence. Your home should be a place where Christ's presence is palpable to all who live and visit there. If guests in your home think, *There's something different about this place*, that means you're doing it right.

For your family, for your neighbors, for your friends—make your home a place people dream about. Make it a place where love, openness, and acceptance are always present; where the practice of presence is like the warmth of a winter stove. Keep the home fires burning.

The truth is, if you aren't practicing presence in your home, you're probably not practicing it at all. Your home is your most important assignment; it may also be your most challenging.

Of course, sometimes the people you love the most are the hardest ones to love. They know everything about you—the good and the bad. They've seen you at your worst, and you've seen them at theirs. This can make it difficult to practice presence. You might think it feels hypocritical to practice presence when these loved ones know

Maybe presence at home
begins with changing
your mind about your
closest relationships.

all your flaws. How can you manifest Christ today when you were kind of a jerk yesterday?

However, consider the voice in your head that makes you hesitate to love your family and reflect God's heart for them. When you hear a voice that suggests you might as well give up on practicing presence at home, whose voice do you think that is? Our enemy understands the danger of a home where presence is practiced—where people grow closer to God and to each other, where prayer is impactful, where sin gets the cold shoulder and selfishness is shunned.

Maybe presence at home begins with changing your mind about your closest relationships. Each time you're about to walk through the door, ask yourself, "Why am I about to walk in? What is God's particular purpose for me in my family's lives? What do they need from me?" Or, more accurately, "What do they need from *Christ* in me?" Consider featuring that word—*presence*—prominently in your home. You'll know what it means. And after a while, so will everyone else.

Home is where the heart is—and presence begins at home.

Several years ago, I (Kerry) was sitting on my front porch with my young son, Grayson. Throughout the years, our times on the porch together have been very special for us.

On this particular occasion I was telling Grayson how frustrated I was about not having an impact on people. I was a pastor with a growing church and had the opportunities to influence many, but I didn't feel like I was having a Christ-inspired impact on people's lives. I didn't feel like I was making a difference.

As I spoke, I saw Grayson listening thoughtfully. After I'd talked for several minutes, he finally interrupted me.

"Dad?" he said slowly. "Don't I count?"

There was silence between us as his question lingered. I realized, perhaps more than ever before, the kind of difference I could and should be making in my own home. I was reminded that even as a pastor—someone who is expected to minister in public—I will never have as much influence anywhere as I have at home.

It's a lesson that has stayed with me. I want the people closest to me to be the ones who respect me the most. I want to influence the ones I hold close; nothing else is more important to me. That's one reason we say presence begins at home.

We know the word "family" can be challenging for some; among us, there are traditional families, single parents, single people who live far away from family, and others in any number of unique circumstances. Regardless of the situation you're in, the idea behind presence in the home is to minister to those closest to you—which can be difficult. Ultimately, your home is your first mission field.

How do you fulfill that mission? First, start with an attitude of prayer and humility. These are perhaps the most powerful tools you have for making meaningful connections at home. According to Scripture, your prayer for your family should be "without ceasing" (1 Thessalonians 5:17). This doesn't mean you have to spend hours praying for your family every day—but it *does* mean you should always be thinking to God about them.

Humility is important because it is your best defense against hypocrisy, which will always surface at home. Those who see you most and know you best must see a person who actually loves Jesus, who doesn't always have to be right, who doesn't insist on having the last word. Selfishness, pride, and control will kill presence.

After humility and prayer, balance at home is key. Be sure family members see you managing your time based on your values. This means that your time commitment to prayer, Bible study, work, leisure, and learning should make godly sense. A more important question than "What's important to you?" is "Based on your calendar for the past month, what's *really* important to you?"

If you really want to live like Jesus, it has to be obvious in your home life. So be like Jesus at home; let his presence in you keep the home fires burning.

In accordance with the "home" theme in this chapter, we're suggesting that the home base for any commitment to presence evangelism consists of five essential promises. These promises are the answer to the question, "Where do I start?" This is why we consider them the starting point for establishing and extending presence evangelism in your life.

We have written each promise in the first person so that, as you read them, you can hear them as promises that *you* are making. If these promises ring true in you, it would be difficult for you *not* to be effective in the practice of presence.

The Five Promises of Presence

1. I promise to love Jesus passionately.

I acknowledge that I have nothing to offer to you unless I am in an intimate relationship with Christ. I know my best-laid plans will crumble to the ground the moment I drift from him. I can do nothing without him and all things through him. What matters most is that I live a life that manifests Christ to everyone around me.

Key text:

"'Teacher, which commandment is the greatest in Moses' Teachings?'

"Jesus answered him, 'Love the Lord your God with all your heart, with all your soul, and with all your mind.' This is the greatest and most important commandment."
(Matthew 22:36–38)

Other texts for study: Deuteronomy 6:5; John 14:21; 1 Corinthians 2:2; Philippians 4:13; 1 John 4:19

2. I promise to love you unconditionally.
My care for you will not be contingent on whether you'll be the person I think you should be or do the things I think you should do. I won't pass judgment on you or impose expectations on you. God accepts you as you are and where you are—and so will I. If I'm doing it right, you will never feel like you have to act different around me—instead, you will feel completely comfortable being exactly who you are.

I will be a loyal friend, someone you can trust. I will be there for you, understanding that's what presence is all about. You are not another notch on my evangelism belt. While I hope and pray that you will someday commit your life to Christ, I will love you as you are right now.

Key text:
> "But if you don't forgive others, your Father will not forgive your failures."
> (Matthew 6:15)

Other texts for study: Luke 6:37; Ephesians 4:32

3. I promise not to stalk or sell.
I promise to respect your boundaries and to refrain from ulterior motives in our relationship. I do care deeply about the condition of your soul; I would be heartless if I didn't. But at the same time, I can't and won't play God in your life.

I will be the kind of person you like being around. I will work hard to be there when you need me, and to give you space when you need it. I will respect you and tell you the truth. I won't try to talk you into anything or spend our time together thinking about the right moment to "pounce."

Key text:
> "A gentle answer turns away rage, but a harsh word stirs up anger."
> (Proverbs 15:1)

Other texts for study: 1 Corinthians 13:4–7; 1 John 3:16

4. I promise to help as best I can.

I acknowledge that friends serve each other, and I will do my best to be helpful as we meet each other's needs and address each other's problems. I won't be lazy or distracted; I will actively ask you how I can help you. To the best of my abilities, I will be selfless in our relationship.

I will always pray for you, because I know that that is by far the most important way I can serve. I know I can't fix everything and would never even try. I'm sure I will disappoint you and I'm guessing you will disappoint me, but through it all, I will be your friend.

Key text:
> "They, too, will ask, 'Lord, when did we see you hungry or thirsty or as a stranger or in need of clothes or sick or in prison and didn't help you?'
> "He will answer them, 'I can guarantee this truth: Whatever you failed to do for one of my brothers or sisters, no matter how unimportant they seemed, you failed to do for me.' These people will go away into eternal punishment, but those with God's approval will go into eternal life."
> (Matthew 25:44–46)

Other texts for study: Mark 12:31; Ephesians 2:10

5. I promise to always be ready to tell you about Jesus.

When the time comes, I promise I won't withhold the truth from you. I'll tell you about what a relationship with Christ is like and why I've chosen it as my lifestyle. While I won't push anything on you, when the time comes, I will not keep quiet about the most important part of my life. I am not ashamed of the gospel and will not be ashamed of Christ when I'm with you. When you have questions about my faith, I will answer as honestly as I can. When I don't know the answer, I'll learn it and respond as soon as I can. I will tell you how you can be saved. I care deeply about your soul. I believe heaven and hell are very real places and that all souls will spend eternity in one or the other—I hope to see you in heaven.

Key text:

> "Jesus answered him, 'I am the way, the truth, and the life. No one goes to the Father except through me.'"
> (John 14:6)

Other texts for study: Acts 8:26–40; 1 Corinthians 15:1–11; 2 Timothy 4:1–4; Romans 1:16-17

PRESENCE PRACTICE

- Which of the Five Promises of Presence is easiest for you to live out? Why?

- Which of the promises is most challenging for you? Why is it challenging? What can you do about it?

- Read Romans 1:16–17: "I'm not ashamed of the Good News. It is God's power to save everyone who believes, Jews first and Greeks as well. God's approval is revealed in this Good News. This approval begins and ends with faith as Scripture says, 'The person who has God's approval will live by faith.'"

- What do you think Romans 1:16–17 has to do with presence evangelism? Why?

- As you consider what presence evangelism might look like in your life, is there a promise you would add to the list above?

6
PRESENCE TOGETHER
❖

As pastors, we believe in the local church. We believe that all who call Christ Lord should be committed members of a Bible-preaching, holiness-loving, community-reaching local church family. We don't think church is optional or secondary; we believe you need the church and the church needs you. Moreover, the practice of presence is part of a healthy life in community.

If there was anyone who could have practiced a life of presence on his own, it was Jesus. After all, he *is* presence. Yet he gathered others around him and charged them with impacting people's lives. He famously told Andrew and Peter, "Come, follow me! I will teach you how to catch people instead of fish" (Matthew 4:19).

This is the nature of the church. Be careful if you're tempted to view presence evangelism as a solitary assignment or if you believe the church is too flawed to be effective. (As someone once said, if you find the perfect church, it won't be once you join.) Even with all its imperfections, the Lord wants the church to thrive:

> Instead, speaking the truth in love, we will grow to become in every respect the mature body of him who is the head, that is, Christ. From him the whole body, joined and held together by

Indeed, the New Testament has no concept of a person who is close to Christ and far from the local church.

every supporting ligament, grows and builds itself up in love,
as each part does its work.
(Ephesians 4:15–16, NIV)

Billy Graham, who declared, "One of the greatest priorities of the
church today is to mobilize the laity to do the work of evangelism,"
also famously said, "Churchgoers are like coals in a fire. When they
cling together, they keep the flame aglow; when they separate, they
die out." Indeed, the New Testament has no concept of a person
who is close to Christ and far from the local church. The "free agent
Christian" is a modern concept (and a modern fallacy).

Furthermore, we see a correspondence between declining commitment to the local church and Christians' declining impact on their
communities. Thom Rainer writes:

> About twenty years ago, a church member was considered
> active in the church if he or she attended three times a week.
> Today, a church member is considered active in the church if
> he or she attends three times a month. Something is wrong
> with this picture. For two thousand years, the local church,
> as messy as it is, has been God's place for believers to gather,
> worship, minister, and be accountable to one another.
>
> And every time I write something about church membership
> and attendance, I inevitably hear cries of "legalism" or "the
> church is not a building" or "the church is a messed-up insti-
> tution." But the local church, the messy local church, is what
> God has used as his primary instrument to make disciples. But
> commitment is waning among many church members.

This, again, is the great irony—people crave connection, yet loneliness spreads. Even as we invent new technologies to foster connection, we are more isolated than ever. The meaningful solution to
all of this loneliness is found in the church. But don't just take our
word for it. As we conclude this chapter, we want to share stories

from people we know who have experienced great restoration through the gift of presence.

To illustrate the power of the local church in presence evangelism, we offer the following story. It's the story of Sharon—someone who caught the vision of presence from our local church—and the friend whose life she helped change. We share this story as an example of the local church's power to cast vision for presence evangelism. Here is the story, shared from the perspective of the friend whose life Sharon helped change.

> I was a desperate woman in a bad situation. Although I had a wonderful family many miles away, my foundation was not built on faith. But then I met Sharon. She became a friend to me in the truest sense of that word. Sharon recognized my lack of foundation and, without any judgment or reservation, simply loved me for who I was and what I was going through.
>
> Sharon's support began with gentle hugs, encouraging words, and prayer. Over time, she started giving me Christian music CDs and making thought-provoking comments like, "There is no such thing as a coincidence." Later, Sharon invited me to Bible studies, church services, and special events. As our friendship flourished, Sharon gave me a copy of the book *Jesus Calling*. In addition to reading the book by myself, I began to read it with Sharon before the workday started; she would say, "Let's start the day in the Word." Though I always *knew* what she meant, I couldn't *feel* what she meant—at least, not at first.
>
> Sharon witnessed to me with grace, purpose, and prophetic hope to face the challenges I was facing. I have never been so appreciative of one person in my whole life. I always knew that Sharon had my back.
>
> I would love to say I was a quick study, but in reality, I was far from it. I waffled in my decisions and behavior. I believed in Jesus, but I wasn't really practicing my faith. Sometimes

I called Sharon crying so hard that she couldn't understand me. Yet Sharon never gave up on me. During those times she simply loved me and prayed with me.

All the while, the seed Sharon had planted so long ago was growing, slowly filling the void in my heart. Our conversations went deeper, and the Lord increasingly revealed himself to me. I began to talk to Jesus more as he became an important part of my day. I celebrated my love for the Lord with Sharon, and she enthusiastically praised him with me. Finally, my faith was part of who I was and who I was supposed to be. The Lord now lives in me and will forever.

I feel overwhelmingly blessed by my friendship with Sharon and the fact that she nurtured the most important relationship in my life. I sometimes wonder how she did it and why she never gave up on me. But the truth is, by discipling me, Sharon was simply listening to God. Like Jesus, she was gentle, patient, and never gave up; she loved me.

Finally, my most important prayer was always for a husband. Now I am about to celebrate my first anniversary with an amazing, godly man. Hallelujah!

 ————————————————————

PRESENCE PRACTICE

Read John 15:9–13 and Proverbs 17:17:

> I have loved you the same way the Father has loved me. So live in my love. If you obey my commandments, you will live in my love. I have obeyed my Father's commandments, and in that way I live in his love. I have told you this so that you will be as joyful as I am, and your joy will be complete. Love each other as I have loved you. This is what I'm commanding you to do. The greatest love you can show is to give your life for your friends.
> (John 15:9–13)

A friend always loves, and a brother is born to share trouble. (Proverbs 17:17)

- Jesus proclaims that the greatest display of love is "to give your life for your friends." Of course, Jesus literally gave his life—he died for his friends. Does he mean for us to do the same? What else might giving your life look like, and what does it have to do with the ministry of presence?

- The Proverbs text says, "A friend always loves." Should we always follow this proverb literally? Why or why not?

- It may be easy to put these scriptures into practice with your Christian friends. But what are the implications for your friendships with nonbelievers? What should those friendships look like?

7
REVIVING COMMUNITY

My (Kerry's) granddaddy was a great cook, and his specialty was homemade yeast rolls. He started from scratch, the old-fashioned way. He called them light rolls because once he had baked a batch, he would seek to be a light in his community by distributing them to the whole neighborhood in Jesus's name.

One day, when a young couple with a small child moved in across the street, Granddaddy hurried into the kitchen to make a batch of light rolls for them. But when he knocked on his neighbors' door to deliver the bread, they treated him quite abruptly, rudely turning him away.

My granddaddy knew about presence long before I did.

As night fell and Granddaddy prepared for bed with a heavy heart, there was a knock on his back door. Standing there in the dim light were his neighbors. With tears in their eyes, they asked his forgiveness for their knee-jerk reaction to his act of kindness.

With trembling lips they asked, "Can we still have the light rolls?" Granddaddy gave them the rolls along with a big smile. From that day forward, those new neighbors were dear friends, and sometimes even asked my granddaddy to babysit their son.

As I was growing up in coastal North Carolina, many of my family members worked as fishermen. But Granddaddy and his light rolls showed me what it meant to be a fisher of men—to live a life of presence and watch the blessings flow!

At our church, we hold an annual men's retreat to North Carolina's Outer Banks. In years past we always stopped at the Chicamacom-ico Life-Saving station, a museum dedicated to the earliest coast guard shore rescuers. Linda, the curator of the museum, would serve as our host as we brought in as many as 100 men to clean, paint, fix the roof, and try to bless the station in whatever way we could. We knew it was a big help for them each spring as they pre-pared for tourism season. And of course, it seemed appropriate that it was a life-saving station.

We always ended our service project by gathering around the origi-nal life-saving boat to hear stories of the rescuers. Finally, we would pray for the people who worked there and go on our way for the rest of the retreat. Linda joined us for those prayers. One year, after we returned from the men's retreat, I received a card in the mail from Linda. She wrote, "I must tell you that long after your group left, the presence of your men still lingered on the grounds of the station."

Of course, the presence she felt was Christ's. But she felt it because of our willingness to be present. Again, you'd be amazed at what God can do through us just *being there*.

There is perhaps nothing that impacts a community more than presence. In fact, the ultimate goal of presence evangelism goes beyond the saving of souls—it extends to the transformation of communities. If you have a vision for impacting your neighborhood, your town, your community—then your presence is critical.

When it comes to the practice of

presence, roll up your sleeves,

fix your gaze on God, and refuse

to be shaken from your pursuit.

Every single soul is worth it.

At our church, that starts with lending a helping hand. Our Hope Distributed ministry provides food, clothing, and even household furnishings to thousands in our community every year. In addition, we have ministries that provide school supplies for kids' outreach into local hospitals. We partner with many helping ministries throughout our town.

But these efforts aren't ends unto themselves. What we want is the privilege of *relationships* in our community. After all, the primary purpose of our lives is to carry the presence of Christ so he can manifest himself through us. Meeting the needs of our community—our neighbors—is a key that unlocks many more opportunities to love, to be a friend, to be there.

In all of this work, the most important thing isn't necessarily what we do or how we do it. Rather, the secret to effective relationships is found in one word: longevity. In fact, we believe longevity is the key to presence evangelism. A long-term commitment communicates love as perhaps nothing else can. In our community, our relationships, and our friendships, we're in it for the long haul. We don't hit and run, and we're not scared off by challenges. Even in our church's overseas outreach, we don't do much that is one time or short term—we stick.

We have already discussed how many people feel about believers. They believe we don't really care, that we always have ulterior motives. Perhaps the most powerful way to combat that perception is by presence—over and over and over again. Patience, endurance, longevity—these are powerful testimonies, and powerful weapons against the enemy.

We remember the story of the abolitionist William Wilberforce (1759–1833), who grew frustrated when he experienced defeat after defeat in his battle against the slave trade. One night Wilberforce opened his Bible and discovered a letter from the great evangelist John Wesley, written shortly before Wesley's death. Wilberforce was strengthened as he read Wesley's words: "Unless the divine power has raised you up, I see not how you can go through your glorious enterprise in opposing that abominable practice of slavery, which is the scandal of religion, of England, and of human nature. Unless God has raised you up for this very thing, you will be worn out by the opposition of men and devils. But if God be for you, who can be against you? Are all of them together stronger than God? Oh, be not weary of well-doing. Go on in the name of God, and in the power of his might."

When it comes to the practice of presence, roll up your sleeves, fix your gaze on God, and refuse to be shaken from your pursuit. Every single soul is worth it.

One of our church members recently shared her experience of being impacted by an individual and a church committed to presence:

> I grew up unchurched, and my husband and I raised our son outside of the church. But in the fall of 2010, my life began to change when the Lord gave me a desire to read and listen to the Bible. My unbelieving friends and family didn't understand this. I couldn't explain it either. But with each passing day, my desire for God's Word grew stronger and stronger.
>
> Then one day a Christian friend talked to me about Jesus and shared what he was doing in her life. When I told her that I was reading the Bible, she told me about a class she was taking at her church. I was very interested, so she made arrangements for me to get my own study workbook.
>
> Weeks later, my friend came by to see me again and I mentioned that I was reading the book of Revelation. She told me her church was offering a class on Revelation and invited me to go. The first time I attended Harrisonburg First Church of the Nazarene, I heard a speaker teach on the end times. The next weekend, I started attending Sunday morning worship

service. Although there were lots of people there, the church never felt like a big church to me—it was more like a family. It was exactly what I needed.

Soon, my friend and I were studying the book of Acts in a Tuesday night ladies' Bible study. It was during that Bible study that I accepted Jesus as my Lord and Savior. When I reflect back on how God worked out all those details, I am so grateful to him and to my Christian friend who loved me enough to lead me to a saving relationship with Jesus Christ.

PRESENCE PRACTICE

Read 2 Peter 1:5–9 and 2 Timothy 4:7–8:

> Because of this, make every effort to add integrity to your faith; and to integrity add knowledge; to knowledge add self-control; to self-control add endurance; to endurance add godliness; to godliness add Christian affection; and to Christian affection add love. If you have these qualities and they are increasing, it demonstrates that your knowledge about our Lord Jesus Christ is living and productive. If these qualities aren't present in your life, you're shortsighted and have forgotten that you were cleansed from your past sins. (2 Peter 1:5–9)

> I have fought the good fight. I have completed the race. I have kept the faith. The prize that shows I have God's approval is now waiting for me. The Lord, who is a fair judge, will give me that prize on that day. He will give it not only to me but also to everyone who is eagerly waiting for him to come again. (2 Timothy 4:7–8)

- Longevity, endurance, and the strength to overcome obstacles are important themes in these passages. In the 2 Peter text, the qualities of endurance, self-control, and godliness are linked together. What is the connection among these three virtues, and what do they have to do with presence?

- In 2 Timothy, why do you think Paul describes faith in terms of a "fight" and a "race"? What point is he making about longevity?

8
YOUR PRESENCE PLAN

In light of all our discussion of presence, what should your plan be? At the heart of presence evangelism is the idea that you don't go into a relationship with guns blazing, ready to coerce someone into getting saved. Instead, you engage the other person with connection and care and work on building a real relationship first, knowing that an opportunity to share the gospel will almost certainly come.

In the well-known text from 1 Corinthians 3, Paul describes the roles we each play in evangelism and discipleship:

> When you are jealous and quarrel among yourselves, aren't you influenced by your corrupt nature and living by human standards? When some of you say, "I follow Paul" and others say, "I follow Apollos," aren't you acting like sinful humans? Who is Apollos? Who is Paul? They are servants who helped you come to faith. Each did what the Lord gave him to do. I planted, and Apollos watered, but God made it grow. So neither the one who plants nor the one who waters is important because only God makes it grow. The one who plants and the one who waters have the same goal, and each will receive a reward for his own work.
> (1 Corinthians 3:3–8)

In the garden of souls, you may not know if or when a friend or family member will commit their lives to Christ. However, you should always be ready for that moment. First Peter 3:15 offers guidance about this: "But dedicate your lives to Christ as Lord. Always be ready to defend your confidence in God when anyone asks you to explain it. However, make your defense with gentleness and respect." Additionally, 2 Timothy 4:2 says, "Be ready to spread the word whether or not the time is right. Point out errors, warn people, and encourage them. Be very patient when you teach."

Of course, these instructions are not easy for everyone. Maybe you feel comfortable with being a friend, listening, or helping someone in need, but when it comes to actually proclaiming the gospel and its role in your life, you feel hesitant. This hesitation usually stems from the idea that you have to "sell" Jesus to the person you're witnessing to, and in the process, risk rejection. You may also worry about knowing exactly what to say when the moment seems right.

To address the first fear, it's important to understand that the saving of souls never has been and never will be up to you. Presence is not about a sales pitch you must master or rejection you must risk. Remember, if you can be a friend, you can practice presence.

Second, it's important to remember that sharing the gospel isn't about becoming a Bible scholar—it's about learning to tell your story. It's important to learn to tell your story in a way that is brief, compelling, and can be delivered at a moment's notice. What the other person does with that story is up to them and the Lord.

We recommend the PRAY model as a method for learning to share the gospel in a way that is short, simple, but also powerful, because it is *your* story. The fact that Jesus has changed your life is the most important tool you have as a presence evangelist. The PRAY model can help you present the gospel through your personal story of faith.

The PRAY Model

P: A description of my past and my problem
Describe what your life was like before your relationship with
Christ, particularly the problems that walking in darkness created
for you. What were you missing before you met the Lord?

R: My encounter with Christ and the beginning of relationship
Talk about how you encountered Jesus. How did you change from
nonbeliever to believer? Did the transformation happen in a singular
moment, or over time? If someone else influenced you in your journey toward repentance, now is the perfect time to tell that story too.

A: A new life in Christ
Describe what your life has been like since you met Jesus. Avoid
the temptation to make everything sound perfect. What do you
have now in the Lord that you were missing previously? This might
include a sense of freedom, peace, acceptance, or community.

Y: What about you?
Invite the other person to respond to your story, whether that invitation is implied ("I just don't know what I would do without him.")
or direct ("I'd love to pray with you right now.").

Kerry's PRAY Testimony

P: A description of my past and my problem
I came to Christ at age twelve. Almost immediately after my initial
repentance, the Lord began to show me the altar again, inviting me
to sign the death warrant of my sinful attitudes. But I held the invitation at arm's length. As a result, I was completely backslidden by
the time I was sixteen. Because I didn't walk in the light, darkness
deceived me. I became a prodigal—I was lost again.

R: My encounter with Christ and the beginning of relationship
As my parents prayed for me, the Holy Spirit came to me again.
Three months into our marriage, my wife, Kim, and I were des-
perate for the Lord. It was obvious to us that something (or rather,

someone) was missing from our lives. We visited a Nazarene church in Harrisonburg, Virginia, and on our second visit, we both came home to God.

A: A new life in Christ
In September 1980, the Lord reclaimed me from my backslidden state and forgave my sins. In August 1987, the Holy Spirit cleansed my heart instantaneously (sanctification). My journey toward wholeness continues as he forms the mind of Christ within me. Now, I know God in ways I never thought I could.

Y: What about you?
My life verse is Philippians 2:13, which says, "It is God who produces in you the desires and actions that please him." That's really what I want. I wouldn't say my life has been perfect since I gave it to Christ, but I have never been without hope or joy—the hope and joy I always longed for. What about you?

Margaret's PRAY Testimony

P: A description of my past and my problem
Growing up in an Old Order Mennonite home, I went to church almost every Sunday. I heard a lot about God in church, but didn't have personal knowledge of his saving grace until later in my life. My own brokenness led me down a long road of bad decisions. The choices I made as a young girl not only hurt me, but my family as well. I fell headlong into rebellion, which led me straight into addiction and deep sin. I was separated from my loved ones and far from God.

R: My encounter with Christ and the beginning of relationship
A few of my clients invited me to church when I cut their hair. They never pushed me but always let me know I was welcome. One day God revealed to me through a piece of his Word (the parable of the sower) that I was a very lost soul. As I thought about finding a church I remembered clients who had been inviting me. They all attended the same church! I started attending with them, and six

months later, at age twenty-nine, I came into a saving relationship with Jesus Christ.

A: A new life in Christ
As I embraced my new relationship with Jesus, my life began to look different. He gave me a clean slate and a new heart. As I began growing in my faith, Jesus not only saved me but also sanctified my heart as I surrendered wholly to him. He has healed my brokenness and freed me from the bondage of addiction. He gives me everything I need for life and for godliness—Christ, the hope of glory.

Y: What about you?
I couldn't keep my newfound freedom in Christ to myself then, and I can't now. I want everyone to know Christ as their Lord and Savior. I pray that Romans 10:15 would be a testimony of my life: "How beautiful are the feet of the messengers who announce the good news!"

In the end, we return to the beginning: the presence of Christ in you must be at the center of your presence to others. The beauty of that truth, of course, is that you can impact people no matter your feelings or circumstances.

More than twenty-five years ago now, I (Kerry) was attending Bible college in Colorado Springs, Colorado. I was working two jobs and going to school four hours a day. Needless to say, life was hectic, and I was sometimes harried.

One of my jobs was working the graveyard shift in the mailroom at Focus on the Family. I was making minimum wage, but with a wife and two small children to support, I was grateful for any work I could get. One night I was particularly weary and honestly didn't feel like going to work. But I pushed myself and went. I walked in that night and put my lunch away in the break room. When I went through the door into the mailroom I saw the janitor, Dave, passing by. I'd only met him once or twice before, but whenever I saw him, he was pushing the same trash can the same way on the same grave-yard shift. Usually we passed each other with few words.

This night, however, Dave asked me, "Kerry, can we please share our meal together at break time tonight?"

I said I would love to. He asked if we could sit on one of the benches and just talk. This had never happened before, and I was curious about his sudden interest in getting together. I asked him what was on his mind.

"When you came through that door," he said excitedly, "I sensed the presence of God all over you."

Of course, I had been tired, bored, and a little frustrated as I went to work that night. *I* didn't feel the presence of God. But Dave did—and it made an impact on him. Christ *in us* is the hope of glory.

This humbling letter from a church member expresses what presence is all about:

> Dear Pastor Margaret,
>
> As I looked up into your serene face last Sunday and saw your bright smile, I felt like I was looking at the face of an angel. And maybe I was. A person in the right place at the right time with the love of Jesus shining straight through her into my heart.
>
> And then as I stood in the emergency room, leaning against the wall, desperately trying to sift through what had just happened and feeling all alone, I stared out to see you walking toward me. You are more than a familiar face. You are a person who seems to understand me, likes me, and has nudged me to show others what is deep inside me, much of which I had kept hidden. You are the person who has taken stands in my life and challenged me to help me grow. How does a person find words to express gratitude for gifts so priceless? The words "thank you" seem so small for gifts so big!

One of the most glorious

benefits of living a life of

presence is the opportunity

to take longevity—

the commitment to

relentless love and friendship—

and turn it into legacy.

On Sunday, the amount of love I absorbed in my heart almost overwhelmed me. It took days for me to process. I wonder if it happened because it was the first time that my heart was healed enough to actually *feel* the love that was directed my way. In the past, I have either felt numbness toward love or redirected it because my heart was not able to absorb it. Maybe I didn't feel I deserved the love. Or maybe I had fenced off corners of my heart, keeping the pain securely under control—not going there myself and not letting anyone else in there, including God. When healing began occurring, there was more room for love to come.

I knew that I was simply babbling in class today, but I was trying to say what I had just discovered. That when one's heart begins to heal and one can finally really feel the love of Jesus, then and only then can one be a powerful witness because then the heart is available for God to shine through in a powerful way. I wondered what was missing in me. I ran around doing good. But now I don't have to run around doing anything. I can just *be* and God will use me in ways he wants—and I don't have to run around like crazy trying to work for him, like any good workaholic would do! My heart is finally free and he can shine straight through me where he wants.

I praise God for giving me this chance to be free in him. How about that for a seventieth birthday present! And I thank you, Pastor Margaret, for your encouragement and your presence and for never giving up on me. Thank you for standing with me, and for coming to the hospital on an afternoon when your precious daughter was in town.

Thank you for sharing your journey with me. Thank you for wanting to use my behind-the-scenes gifts as the plan for relational outreach is developed. You have given and are giving me something very valuable—something I either never had before or had and could not feel.

Finally, I thank you for doing what you have done for me so that I was ready and could take in the magnitude of Jesus's gifts for me.

One of the most glorious benefits of living a life of presence is the opportunity to take longevity—the commitment to relentless love and friendship—and turn it into legacy. My (Kerry's) godly grandmother, Granny Margery, was powerfully present in my life and allowed the Holy Spirit to minister to me through her. For this reason, her influence on me was unfathomable. Since she has been absent from the body (and without doubt is now present with the Lord), the Holy Spirit continues to minister to me through the unforgettable afterglow of Granny's life. Living a life of presence means Jesus can make an impact through you long after you are gone.

And now it's your turn to build the same kind of legacy—to fulfill the Great Commission by living a life of presence. As you do so, who knows how many souls you will impact for Christ? We pray that the Spirit will go with you as you seek to carry his presence into the world.

PRESENCE PRACTICE

Take some time to work on your PRAY testimony—we suggest that you write it down. Get used to talking about your encounter with Christ, your salvation experience, and your life in a way that is meaningful and easy to understand. You don't have to add any drama or exaggerate—just tell your story. In the context of relationships, it can and will be life-saving for many.

P: A description of my past and my problem

_____

_____

_____

_____

_____

_____

_____

_____

R: My encounter with Christ and the beginning of relationship

_____

_____

_____

_____

_____

_____

A: A new life in Christ

_____

_____

_____

_____

_____

_____

_____

_____

Y: What about you?

_____

_____

_____

_____

_____

_____

_____